HOW DO I BUILD A HEALTHY FAMILY?

JOHN RAGSDALE

How Do I Build a Healthy Family?

Cover design by Kim Russell | Wahoo Designs

ISBN: 978-0-9997706-2-7

ABOUT THE AUTHOR

John Ragsdale is a husband to Kristin, a dad to Evan and Davis, a singer-songwriter, a passionate communicator, and pastor of The Hills Nashville. John feels called to encourage people to be all that God created them to be.

@johnrags [twitter & instagram] • johnragsdale.org [website]
thehillsnashville.com

CONTENTS

A MESSAGE TO READERS

Your family is a priceless gift from your Father in heaven. What will you do with that gift? Will you do your best to create a loving home that honors the Creator and His only begotten Son? Will you treat your family members with respect, courtesy, patience, understanding, and forgiveness? Will you make the Golden Rule the blueprint by which you build lifelong family ties? Of course you should, and with God's help, you can.

This text contains biblically based principles that can help you build a healthier, happier family. The ideas on these pages are common-sense tools which will help you build your family's collective life upon the only foundation that can never be shaken—the foundation of God's Holy Word.

God's promises are found in a book like no other: the Holy Bible. As a Christian, you understand the need to trust God's promises, to follow His commandments, and to share the Good News of His Son. So, as you and your family members face the inevitable challenges of everyday life—the ups, the downs, and the complications of surviving and striving in the twenty-first century—you must arm yourselves with the promises and principles found in God's Word. When you do, you and your loved ones can expect the best, not only for the day ahead or for the week ahead or for the year ahead, but for all eternity.

SEVEN STEPS TO A HEALTHIER FAMILY

Put God First. A healthy family is inevitably built upon a strong spiritual foundation. In the life of every Christian family, God should come first. No exceptions.

Establish Proper Priorities. Whether you realize it or not, your world is brimming with dangerous distractions and time-wasting temptations. So your task is to distance yourself from unnecessary distractions by establishing clear priorities and focusing on important matters first, and making ample time for your family.

Be Obedient. You and your family members are more likely to sense God's guidance—and more likely to hear His voice—when you're walking in the light and obeying His commandments. When you're obedient, you'll receive countless blessings that you would have missed if you'd ignored God's commandments.

Be Quick to Forgive. None of us are perfect, so all of us need forgiveness from time to time. The sooner you can forgive those who have hurt you—including your family members—the healthier your family will be.

Make Prayer an Essential Part of Your Family's Life. As the old saying goes, "The family that prays together stays together." And the family that prays together stays healthier too.

Avoid Angry Outbursts. Unfettered anger can be dangerous to a family's health. Guard your words—and your heart—accordingly.

Trust God and Be Optimistic. As a Christian, you have every reason to be optimistic about your life here on earth and your eternal life in heaven. So stay hopeful, optimistic, and upbeat. You'll be blessed by your positive attitude, and your family will be blessed too.

1

THE QUESTION

I desperately want to have a healthy family.
Where do I start?

THE ANSWER

The perfect place to start is by opening—and studying—a book that you already own: the Holy Bible. God's Word contains clear instructions which, if followed, can help you build a stronger family and a better life.

The God who adopted you into His forever family knows how to make earthly families work.

CHARLES STANLEY

YOUR FAMILY IS A GIFT FROM GOD

Choose for yourselves this day whom you will serve. . . . But as for me and my house, we will serve the Lord.

Joshua 24:15 NKJV

A loving family is a treasure from God. If God has blessed you with a close knit, supportive clan, offer a word of thanks to your Creator because He has given you one of His most precious earthy possessions. Your obligation, in response to God's gift, is to treat your family in ways that are consistent with His commandments.

You live in a fast-paced, demanding world, a place where life can be difficult and pressures can be intense. As those pressures build, you may tend to focus so intently upon your obligations that you lose sight, albeit temporarily, of your spiritual and emotional needs. That's one reason why a regular daily devotional time is so important: It offers a badly needed dose of perspective.

Even when the demands of everyday life are great, you must never forget that you have been entrusted with a profound responsibility—the responsibility of contributing to your family's emotional and spiritual wellbeing. It's a big job, but with God's help, you're up to the task.

When you place God squarely in the center of your family's life—when you worship Him, praise Him, trust Him, and love Him—then He will most certainly bless you and yours in ways that you could have scarcely imagined. So the next time your family life becomes a little stressful, remember this: That little band of men, women, kids, and babies is a priceless treasure on temporary loan from the Father above. And it's your responsibility to praise God for that gift, and to act accordingly.

MORE FROM GOD'S WORD

But now abide faith, hope, love, these three;
but the greatest of these is love.

1 Corinthians 13:13 NKJV

Their first responsibility is to show godliness at home
and repay their parents by taking care of them.
This is something that pleases God.

1 Timothy 5:4 NLT

Better a dry crust with peace
than a house full of feasting with strife.

Proverbs 17:1 HCSB

Every kingdom divided against itself is headed for
destruction, and a house divided against itself falls.

Luke 11:17 HCSB

But if anyone does not provide for his own,
and especially for those of his household, he has
denied the faith and is worse than an unbeliever.

1 Timothy 5:8 NASB

MORE THOUGHTS ABOUT FAMILY

Apart from religious influence, the family
is the most important influence on society.

Billy Graham

I like to think of my family as a big, beautiful
patchwork quilt—each of us so different yet
stitched together by love and life experiences.

Barbara Johnson

The secret of a happy home life
is that the members of the family
learn to give and receive love.

Billy Graham

There is so much compassion and understanding
that is gained when we've experienced God's
grace firsthand within our own families.

Lisa Whelchel

Money can build or buy a house. Add love to that,
and you have a home. Add God to that,
and you have a temple. You have
"a little colony of the kingdom of heaven."

Anne Ortlund

REMEMBER THIS

If you're experiencing tough times, don't be afraid to seek help. If you're facing family problems that you just can't seem to solve, don't hesitate to consult your pastor or an experienced family counselor.

GET PRACTICAL

Let your family members know that you love them by the things you say and the things you do. Every time you enjoy a meal with your family, you have yet another opportunity to express your love and appreciation for them. And that's precisely what you should do.

A CONVERSATION STARTER

Talk to a friend about your family: it's strengths and weaknesses. Talk about simple strategies you can employ to build upon those strengths and correct some of the weaknesses.

NOTES TO YOURSELF ABOUT YOUR AMILY AS A GIFT FROM GOD

Write down specific steps you can take to strengthen your family ties and improve familial relationships.

2

THE QUESTION

I'd like to have more family time, but I'm swamped. There's simply not enough time in the day for me to get everything done. What should I do?

THE ANSWER

God wants you to understand His priorities and act accordingly. But if you lose perspective, God's Word instructs you to slow down, to calm down, and to pray. When you ask God to put first things first, He will do it.

Wife and family come before business, ministry, or career. God comes before wife and family.

Edwin Louis Cole

ESTABLISHING THE RIGHT PRIORITIES

Therefore, whether you eat or drink, or whatever you do, do everything for God's glory.

1 Corinthians 10:31 HCSB

First things first." These words are easy to speak but hard to put into practice. For busy people living in a demanding world, placing first things first can be difficult indeed, especially when it comes to spending high-quality time with our families. There's so much to do and our calendars are so full.

If you're having trouble prioritizing your day, perhaps you've been trying to organize your life according to your own plans, not God's. A better strategy, of course, is to take your daily obligations and place them in the hands of the One who created you. To do so, you must prioritize your day according to God's commandments, and you must seek His will and His wisdom in all matters.

Have you fervently asked God to help prioritize your day and your life? Have you asked Him for guidance and for the courage to do the things that you know need to be done? If so, then you're continually inviting your Creator to reveal Himself in a variety of ways. As a follower of Christ, you must do no less.

When you make God's priorities your priorities, you will receive God's abundance and His peace. When you allow God to reign over your heart, He will honor you with spiritual blessings that are simply too numerous to count. So, as you plan for the day ahead, make God's will your ultimate priority. When you do, every other priority—including the priorities you establish for your family—will become clear.

MORE FROM GOD'S WORD

He who trusts in his riches will fall,
but the righteous will flourish.

PROVERBS 11:28 NASB

For where your treasure is,
there your heart will be also.

LUKE 12:34 HCSB

But prove yourselves doers of the word,
and not merely hearers who delude themselves.

JAMES 1:22 NASB

Trust in the LORD with all your heart
and lean not on your own understanding.

PROVERBS 3:5 NIV

In every way be an example
of doing good deeds. When you teach,
do it with honesty and seriousness.

TITUS 2:7 HCSB

MORE THOUGHTS ABOUT PRIORITIES

For whatever life holds for you and your family in the coming days, weave the unfailing fabric of God's Word through your heart and mind. It will hold strong, even if the rest of life unravels.

Gigi Graham Tchividjian

While you can't do much about your ancestors, you can influence your descendants greatly.

John Maxwell

You have heard about "quality time" and "quantity time." Your family needs both.

Jim Gallery

Never give your family the leftovers and crumbs of your time.

Charles Swindoll

REMEMBER THIS

No matter how busy you are, God wants you to make time for your family. When you make family time a top priority, you'll be blessed and so well they.

GET PRACTICAL

To establish priorities, you can use planning calendars, lists, and bulletin boards. That way, you can keep everybody in your family informed of what's going on and who's doing what. Far more families suffer from underplanning than from overplanning.

A CONVERSATION STARTER

Talk to a friend about your priorities: what they are and what they should be.

NOTES TO YOURSELF ABOUT PRIORITIES

Write down your most important family-related priorities. Then, jot down specific steps you can take to fulfill any unmet obligations to your family.

3

THE QUESTION

I know that God wants me to love my family.
But what, specifically, does He want me to do?

THE ANSWER

Familial love should be demonstrated with deeds, not just announced with words. You demonstrate your love by giving of yourself and your time. While you're with your loved ones, be sure to watch carefully and listen with your ears, your eyes, and your heart.

The first essential for a happy home is love.

Billy Graham

AND THE GREATEST OF THESE.

And now abide faith, hope, love, these three; but the greatest of these is love.

1 Corinthians 13:13 NKJV

Christ's words are clear: we are to love God first, and secondly, we are to love others as we love ourselves (Matthew 22:37–40). These two commands are seldom easy, and because we are imperfect beings, we often fall short. But God's Holy Word commands us to try.

The Christian path is an exercise in love and forgiveness. If we are to walk in Christ's footsteps, we must forgive those who have done us harm, and we must accept Christ's love by sharing it freely with family, friends, neighbors, and even strangers.

God does not intend for you to experience mediocre relationships; He created you for far greater things. Building lasting relationships requires compassion, wisdom, empathy, kindness, courtesy, and forgiveness. If that sounds like a lof of work, it is—which is perfectly fine with God. Why? Because He knows that you are capable of doing that work, and because He knows that the fruits of your labors will enrich the lives of your loved ones and the lives of generations yet unborn.

Do you love your family? Of course you do. Your family is God's gift to you, and it's up to you to treat that gift with the respect, the honor, and the love that it deserves. The Bible teaches that love is a fruit of the Spirit. So make sure that everyone in your family can see—by your actions and by your words—that the spirit of love continues to grow and flourish in your heart. When you do, you'll make everybody happy, including the person you see every time you look in the mirror.

MORE FROM GOD'S WORD

And we have known and believed the love that God has for us. God is love, and he who abides in love abides in God, and God in him.

1 John 4:16 NKJV

Above all, love each other deeply, because love covers a multitude of sins.

1 Peter 4:8 NIV

Beloved, if God so loved us, we ought also to love one another.

1 John 4:11 KJV

A new commandment I give unto you, That ye love one another; as I have loved you, that ye also love one another.

John 13:34 KJV

Love is patient, love is kind. Love does not envy, is not boastful, is not conceited.

1 Corinthians 13:4 HCSB

MORE THOUGHTS ABOUT LOVE

Carve your name on hearts, not on marble.

C. H. SPURGEON

Love must be supported and fed and protected, just like a little infant who is growing up at home.

JAMES DOBSON

Brotherly love is still the distinguishing badge of every true Christian.

MATTHEW HENRY

It matters that we should be true to one another, be loyal to what is a family—only a little family in the great Household, but still a family, with family love alive in it and action as a living bond.

AMY CARMICHAEL

When you think about it for a moment, it certainly makes sense that if people can establish a loving and compatible relationship at home, they have a better chance of establishing winning relationships with those with whom they work on a regular basis.

ZIG ZIGLAR

REMEMBER THIS

It helps to be expressive. So make certain that at your house, love is expressed and demonstrated many times each day. Little acts of consideration and kindness can make a big difference in the way that your loved ones feel and the way your loved ones respond.

GET PRACTICAL

Today and every day, look for creative ways to demonstrate the love that you feel for your family. Small gestures of love and brief words of encouragement can make a big difference in the life of your family. So don't wait for tomorrow. Give practical demonstrations of your love today.

A CONVERSATION STARTER

Talk to a friend about simple, straightforward ways that you can demonstrate the love that you feel for your family. Focus, not just on words, but also on tangible steps you can take to be more compassionate and kind to your loved ones.

NOTES TO YOURSELF ABOUT WAYS TO EXPRESS YOUR LOVE

Write down specific things you can do to express your love to members of your immediate family. Focus on things you can do today, tomorrow, or in the next few days.

4

THE QUESTION

This world is a crazy place, and sometimes it's very hard for me and my family members to be obedient Christians. What does the Bible say about obedience?

THE ANSWER

God's word is clear: we must obey Him or face the consequences. The Lord rewards obedience and punishes disobedience. So, it's not enough to understand His rules; we must also live by them. The more carefully we study God's Word—and the more closely we follow in the footsteps of His Son—the happier and healthier we'll be.

A man ought to live so that everybody knows he is a Christian, and most of all, his family ought to know.

D. L. Moody

IT PAYS TO OBEY

Now by this we know that we know Him,
if we keep His commandments.
1 John 2:3 NKJV

God has given us a guidebook for abundant life; that book is the Holy Bible. It contains thorough instructions which, if followed, lead to fulfillment, righteousness, and salvation. But, if we choose to ignore God's commandments, the results are as predictable as they are tragic.

How can we demonstrate our love for God? By placing Christ squarely at the center of our lives. Jesus said that if we are to love Him, we must obey His commandments (John 14:15). Thus, our obedience to the Master is an expression of our love for Him.

In Ephesians 2:10 we read, "For we are His workmanship, created in Christ Jesus for good works." (NKJV). These words are instructive: we are not saved by good works, but for good works. Good works are not the root, but rather the fruit of our salvation.

When we seek righteousness in our own lives—and when we seek the companionship of those who do likewise—we reap the spiritual rewards that God intends for our lives. When we behave ourselves as godly people, we honor God. When we live righteously and according to God's commandments, He blesses us in ways that we cannot fully understand.

As families, we should take every step of our journey with the Lord. We should continue to read His Word and we should continue to follow His commandments. We should support only those activities that further His kingdom and our own spiritual growth. And we should be worthy examples to our friends and neighbors. When we do, we'll reap the blessings that God has promised to all those who live according to His will and His Word.

MORE FROM GOD'S WORD

But prove yourselves doers of the word, and not merely hearers who delude themselves.

JAMES 1:22 NASB

Praise the LORD! Happy are those who respect the LORD, who want what he commands.

PSALM 112:1 NCV

Trust in the LORD with all your heart, and lean not on your own understanding; in all your ways acknowledge Him, and He shall direct your paths.

PROVERBS 3:5–6 NKJV

We must obey God rather than men.

ACTS 5:29 NASB

Teach me, O LORD, the way of Your statutes, and I shall observe it to the end.

PSALM 119:33 NASB

MORE THOUGHTS ABOUT OBEDIENCE

Examine yourselves—ask, each of you, "Have I been a good brother?...son? ... husband?... father?...servant?"

CHARLES KINGSLEY

Happiness is obedience and obedience is happiness

C. H. SPURGEON

The golden rule for understanding in spiritual matters is not intellect, but obedience.

OSWALD CHAMBERS

Obedience is the key to every door.

GEORGE MACDONALD

Faith and obedience are bound up in the same bundle. He that obeys God, trusts God; and he that trusts God, obeys God.

C. H. SPURGEON

REMEMBER THIS

Because God is just, He rewards good behavior just as surely as He punishes sin. Obedience earns God's pleasure; disobedience doesn't.

GET PRACTICAL

Reading God's Word can help you stay on the proper path: His path. When you study the Bible every day, you'll find it easier to be obedient.

A CONVERSATION STARTER

Talk to a friend about the rewards of obedience and the dangers of disobedience. While you're at it, consider the various temptations and distractions that are woven into the fabric of everyday life.

NOTES TO YOURSELF ABOUT OBEDIENCE

Write down a few thoughts about the rewards of obeying God's laws and the dangers of disobeying them.

5

THE QUESTION

What should Christ's love mean to me?

THE ANSWER

Christ's love should be the cornerstone of your life and your family. Jesus gave His life so that you and your loved ones might live forever with Him in heaven. And how can you repay Christ's love? By accepting Him into your heart and following, as best you can, in His footsteps.

Live your lives in love, the same sort of love which Christ gives us, and which He perfectly expressed when He gave Himself as a sacrifice to God.

Corrie ten Boom

YOUR FAMILY'S RELATIONSHIP WITH JESUS

As the Father loved Me,
I also have loved you; abide in My love.

JOHN 15:9 NKJV

Jesus loves your family so much that He endured unspeakable suffering for you and your loved ones. How will you respond to Christ's sacrifice? Will you take up your cross and follow Him (Luke 9:23) or will you choose another path? When you place your hopes squarely at the foot of the cross—and when you place Jesus squarely at the center of your home life—you will be blessed.

The nineteenth-century writer Hannah Whitall Smith observed, "The crucial question for each of us is this: What do you think of Jesus, and do you yet have a personal acquaintance with Him?" This question applies not only to you, but also to your clan.

Thomas Brooks spoke for believers of every generation when he observed, "Christ is the sun, and all the watches of our lives should be set by the dial of his motion." Christ, indeed, is the ultimate savior of mankind and the personal savior of those who believe in Him. As his servants, we should place Him at the very center of our lives and at the center of our households. When we do, we are blessed today, tomorrow, and throughout eternity.

MORE FROM GOD'S WORD

For God so loved the world, that he gave his only begotten Son, that whosoever believeth in him should not perish, but have everlasting life.

John 3:16 KJV

We love him, because he first loved us.

1 John 4:19 KJV

For Christ also suffered once for sins, the just for the unjust, that He might bring us to God, being put to death in the flesh but made alive by the Spirit.

1 Peter 3:18 NKJV

I am the good shepherd. The good shepherd lays down his life for the sheep.

John 10:11 HCSB

No one has greater love than this, that someone would lay down his life for his friends.

John 15:13 HCSB

MORE THOUGHTS ABOUT RELATIONSHIP WITH JESUS

The only source of Life is the Lord Jesus Christ.

OSWALD CHAMBERS

Above all else, the Christian life
is a love affair of the heart.

JOHN ELDREDGE

Jesus is all compassion. He never betrays us.

CATHERINE MARSHALL

Jesus: the proof of God's love.

PHILLIP YANCEY

As the love of a husband for his bride,
such is the love of Christ for His people.

C. H. SPURGEON

REMEMBER THIS

Christ's love is amazing and eternal. His love can—and should—be the cornerstone and the touchstone of your relationship with Jesus.

GET PRACTICAL

An old hymn begins, "What a friend we have in Jesus." How true. Jesus is, indeed, the sovereign friend and ultimate savior of mankind. He is the light of the world. Today and every day, make sure that you are capturing and reflecting His light.

A CONVERSATION STARTER

Talk to a friend about what it means to for your family to have relationship with Jesus.

NOTES TO YOURSELF ABOUT YOUR FAMILY'S RELATIONSHIP WITH JESUS.

Write down your thoughts about how your family's life has been changed by their relationship with Jesus.

6

THE QUESTION

I know that our family should probably pray more, but it seems like we never get around to it. What does the Bible say about prayer, and how will the quality of my family's prayer life impact our lives?

THE ANSWER

God's Word teaches us that prayer is an essential part of a well-lived life. One way to make sure that your family is in tune with God is to pray often. The more you and your loved ones talk to Him, the more He will talk to you.

It is impossible to overstate the need for prayer in the fabric of family life.

JAMES DOBSON

THE POWER OF PRAYER IN THE LIFE OF YOUR FAMILY

Rejoice always, pray without ceasing, in everything give thanks; for this is the will of God in Christ Jesus for you.

1 Thessalonians 5:16–18 NKJV

Does prayer play an important role in the life of your family? Is prayer an integral part of your daily routine or is it a hit-or-miss activity? Do you "pray without ceasing," or is your prayer life an afterthought? If you genuinely wish to receive the abundant life that is available through Christ, you must pray constantly, and you must never underestimate the power of prayer.

As you contemplate the quality of your family's prayer life, here are a few things to consider: 1. God hears our prayers and answers them (Jeremiah 29:11–12). 2. God promises that the prayers of righteous people can accomplish great things (James 5:16). 3. God invites us to be still and to feel His presence (Psalm 46:10).

So pray. Pray as a family and pray individually. Start praying in the early morning and keep praying until you fall off to sleep at night. Pray about matters great and small; and be watchful for the answers that God most assuredly sends your way.

Daily prayer and meditation is a matter of will and habit. When you organize you day to include quiet moments with God, you'll soon discover that no time is more precious than the silent moments you spend with Him.

The quality of your spiritual life will be in direct proportion to the quality of your prayer life. So do yourself and your loved ones a favor: instead of turning things over in your mind, turn them over to God in prayer. Instead of worrying about your next decision, ask God to lead the way. Don't limit your prayers to meals or to bedtime. Pray constantly because God is listening—and He wants to hear from you. And without question, you need to hear from Him.

MORE FROM GOD'S WORD

Ask and it will be given to you; seek and you will find; knock and it will be opened to you. For everyone who asks receives, and he who seeks finds, and to him who knocks it will be opened.

Matthew 7:7–8 NASB

And whenever you stand praying,
if you have anything against anyone,
forgive him, so that your Father in heaven
may also forgive you your wrongdoing.

Mark 11:25 HCSB

Confess your trespasses to one another,
and pray for one another, that you may be healed.
The effective, fervent prayer
of a righteous man avails much.

James 5:16 NKJV

I desire therefore that the men pray everywhere,
lifting up holy hands, without wrath and doubting.

1 Timothy 2:8 NKJV

MORE THOUGHTS ABOUT PRAYER

The most effective thing we can do for our children and families is to pray for them.

ANTHONY EVANS

The vast ocean of Love cannot be measured or explained, but it can be experienced.

SARAH YOUNG

Love always means sacrifice.

ELISABETH ELLIOT

Line by line, moment by moment, special times are etched into our memories in the permanent ink of everlasting love in our relationships.

GLORIA GAITHER

The family that prays together, stays together.

OLD SAYING

REMEMBER THIS

If you're having troubles of any sort, pray about them. Prayer changes things, and it changes you. And prayer can make dramatic improvements in the life of your family. So pray.

GET PRACTICAL

If you can't seem to hear God, go to a quiet place, and ask for His help. If you ask, and keep asking, He'll heal your heart and guide your path.

A CONVERSATION STARTER

Talk to a friend about your experiences concerning prayer: times when your prayer life was meaningful and times when you found it hard to pray. How did the quality and quantity of your prayers impact the other members of your family?

NOTES TO YOURSELF ABOUT PRAYER

Write down your thoughts about the power of prayer, the need for prayer, and the impact that your own prayer life has on the people you care for.

7

THE QUESTION

It's a complicated world, and we're getting lots of mixed messages. I know that my family members and I should seek God's guidance. How do we do that?

THE ANSWER

If you and your loved ones learn to consult God early and often, you'll be blessed. So when you're about to make an important decision, remember that God's Word is the final word. And if you want God's guidance, ask for it. When you pray for guidance, and listen carefully for His response, He will lead you in a direction of His choosing.

Walk in the daylight of God's will because then you will be safe; you will not stumble.

ANNE GRAHAM LOTZ

SEEKING GOD'S GUIDANCE

Trust in the LORD with all your heart, and lean not on your own understanding; in all your ways acknowledge Him, and He shall direct your paths.

PROVERBS 3:5–6 NKJV

As Christians we have every reason to live joyously and courageously. After all, Christ has already fought and won our battle for us—He did so on the cross at Calvary. But despite Christ's sacrifice, and despite God's promises, we may become confused or disoriented by the endless complications and countless distractions of life in the twenty-first century.

C. S. Lewis observed, "I don't doubt that the Holy Spirit guides your decisions from within when you make them with the intention of pleasing God. The error would be to think that He speaks only within, whereas in reality He speaks also through Scripture, the Church, Christian friends, and books." These words remind us that God has many ways to make Himself known. Our challenge is to make ourselves open to His instruction.

Do you place a high value on God's guidance, and do you talk to Him regularly about matters great and small? Or do you talk with God on a haphazard basis? If you're wise, you'll form the habit of speaking to God early and often. But you won't stop there—you'll also study God's Word, you'll obey God's commandments, and you'll associate with people who do likewise.

So, if you're unsure of your next step, lean upon God's promises and lift your prayers to Him. Remember that God is always near—always trying to get His message through. Open yourself to Him every day, and trust Him to guide your path.

When you do, your family life will improve, and you'll be protected today, tomorrow, and forever.

MORE FROM GOD'S WORD

Morning by morning he wakens me and opens my understanding to his will. The Sovereign LORD has spoken to me, and I have listened.

ISAIAH 50:4–5 NLT

Shew me thy ways, O LORD; teach me thy paths.
Lead me in thy truth, and teach me:
for thou art the God of my salvation;
on thee do I wait all the day.

PSALM 25:4–5 KJV

Teach me to do Your will, for You are my God; Your Spirit is good. Lead me in the land of uprightness.

PSALM 143:10 NKJV

Yet LORD, You are our Father;
we are the clay, and You are our potter;
we all are the work of Your hands.

ISAIAH 64:8 HCSB

The LORD says, "I will guide you
along the best pathway for your life.
I will advise you and watch over you."

PSALM 32:8 NLT

MORE THOUGHTS ABOUT SEEKING GOD'S GUIDANCE

A family is a place where principles are hammered and honed on the anvil of everyday living.

CHARLES SWINDOLL

*When we are obedient,
God guides our steps and our stops.*

CORRIE TEN BOOM

God never leads us to do anything that is contrary to the Bible.

BILLY GRAHAM

Are you serious about wanting God's guidance to become a personal reality in your life? The first step is to tell God that you know you can't manage your own life; that you need his help.

CATHERINE MARSHALL

A home is a place where we find direction.

GIGI GRAHAM TCHIVIDJIAN

REMEMBER THIS

God has a perfect plan for your life, and He can handle every challenge you face. You can trust Him to manage every aspect of your life, including your family life.

GET PRACTICAL

When you decide, once and for all, to allow God to guide your family life, other decisions will have a way of falling into place. You and your family members make countless decisions each day. When you seek God's guidance—and when you make decisions based upon the unchanging principles of His Holy Word—you'll decide wisely.

A CONVERSATION STARTER

Talk to a friend about specific ways you can hear God's voice and follow His path.

NOTES TO YOURSELF ABOUT THE DIRECTION GOD IS LEADING YOU

Write down some of the things you feel God is calling you to do this week, this month, and this year.

8

THE QUESTION

I know I should be kind to everybody, starting with the members of my own family. But sometimes it's hard to overlook the obvious personality flaws of people who stretch my patience to the limit. What does the Bible instruct me to do?

THE ANSWER

The Bible teaches us to treat all people as we would wish to be treated if we were in their shoes. It's hard, but not impossible, to treat everybody with respect, even the kids and grownups who try our patience.

The Golden Rule begins at home.

Marie T. Freeman

MAKING THE GOLDEN RULE YOUR FAMILY'S RULE

Therefore, whatever you want men to do to you, do also to them, for this is the Law and the Prophets.

Matthew 7:12 NKJV

Is the Golden Rule one of the rules that governs your household? Hopefully so. Obeying the Golden Rule is a proven way to improve all your relationships, including your relationships with the people who happen to live inside the four walls of your home. But the reverse is also true: if you or your loved ones ignore the Golden Rule, you're headed for trouble, and fast.

Jesus taught us that we should treat other people (including our family members) in the same way that we want to be treated. That's the Golden Rule. Yet sometimes, especially when we're feeling pressured, tired, or upset, obeying the Golden Rule can seem like an impossible task—but it's not.

God's Word makes it clear: we are to treat our loved ones with respect, kindness, fairness, and courtesy. And He knows we can do so if we try. So if you're wondering how you should treat your loved ones—or anybody else, for that matter—just ask the person you see every time you look into the mirror. The answer you receive will tell you exactly what to do.

MORE FROM GOD'S WORD

Do nothing out of rivalry or conceit, but in humility consider others as more important than yourselves.

PHILIPPIANS 2:3 HCSB

Who is wise and understanding among you? Let him show by good conduct that his works are done in the meekness of wisdom.

JAMES 3:13 NKJV

Let us not become weary in doing good, for at the proper time we will reap a harvest if we do not give up.

GALATIANS 6:9 NIV

A good person produces good things from the treasury of a good heart, and an evil person produces evil things from the treasury of an evil heart. What you say flows from what is in your heart.

LUKE 6:45 NLT

Verily I say unto you, Inasmuch as ye have done it unto one of the least of these my brethren, ye have done it unto me.

MATTHEW 25:40 KJV

MORE THOUGHTS ABOUT THE GOLDEN RULE

It is one of the most beautiful compensations of life that no one can sincerely try to help another without helping herself.

BARBARA JOHNSON

Love is not grabbing, or self-centered, or selfish. Real love is being able to contribute to the happiness of another person without expecting to get anything in return.

JAMES DOBSON

Faith never asks whether good works are to be done, but has done them before there is time to ask the question, and it is always doing them.

MARTIN LUTHER

You can't light another's path without casting light on your own.

JOHN MAXWELL

Do all the good you can, by all the means you can, in all the ways you can, in all the places you can, at all the times you can, to all the people you can, as long as ever you can.

JOHN WESLEY

REMEMBER THIS

The Golden Rule should begin within the four walls of your own home. If your family members can't follow God's rule at home, they'll most certainly have trouble obeying it anyplace else.

GET PRACTICAL

You have a big role to play in helping to maintain a peaceful home. It's a big job, so don't be afraid to ask for help . . . especially God's help.

A CONVERSATION STARTER

Talk to a friend about the rewards of living the Golden Rule in your family.

NOTES TO YOURSELF ABOUT THE GOLDEN RULE

Write down your thoughts about practical ways to apply the Golden Rule in dealing with members of your family.

9

THE QUESTION

What does God's Word say
about stewardship and generosity?

THE ANSWER

The Bible teaches us to serve the Lord with gladness. So, faithful Christian service and stewardship should be woven into the very fabric of family life. Every member of your family possesses special abilities and unique opportunities to serve. Whether you realize it or not, God has called you to a life of service. Your job is to find a place to serve and to get busy.

Whole-life stewardship means putting
the purposes of God at the
very center of our lives and families.

Tom Sine

BEING GOOD STEWARDS OF YOUR FAMILY'S RESOURCES

As each one has received a gift,
minister it to one another, as good stewards
of the manifold grace of God.

1 Peter 4:10 NKJV

Christian stewardship may be defined as "the proper management of one's resources for the glory of God." And for thoughtful believers, stewardship isn't a hit or miss proposition, it's a way of thinking and a way of living.

As Christians, we are challenged to be faithful stewards of the resources and talents that God has given us. But we live in a world that encourages us to do otherwise. Ours is a society that is filled to the brim with countless opportunities to squander our time, our talents, our energy, and our money. But we must beware: God warns us not to waste the blessings that He has bestowed upon us, and we must heed that warning.

Every member of your family possesses special gifts, unique talents and opportunities that can be used or not. You should value the talents that God has given you, you should nourish those talents, and you should share them with the world.

For dedicated Christian families like yours, stewardship is not something to be taken lightly. After all, God has given you countless blessings. That's why you must manage your family's resources as if they were vitally important to God, which, by the way, they are.

MORE FROM GOD'S WORD

Make a joyful noise unto the Lord,
all ye lands. Serve the Lord with gladness:
come before his presence with singing.

PSALM 100:1–2 KJV

Whatever you do, do your work heartily, as for the Lord rather than for men.

COLOSSIANS 3:23 NASB

But each person should examine his own work, and then he will have a reason for boasting in himself alone, and not in respect to someone else. For each person will have to carry his own load.

GALATIANS 6:4–5 HCSB

His master replied, "Well done, good and faithful servant! You have been faithful with a few things; I will put you in charge of many things. Come and share your master's happiness!"

MATTHEW 25:21 NIV

Be diligent that ye may be found of him in peace, without spot, and blameless.

2 PETER 3:14 KJV

MORE THOUGHTS ABOUT STEWARDSHIP

A steward is one who manages another's resources. Each of us is a manager, not an owner. God is the owner, and we are to manage according to His plan.

LARRY BURKETT

Our voices, our service, and our abilities are to be employed, primarily, for the glory of God.

BILLY GRAHAM

God wants us to serve Him with a willing spirit, one that would choose no other way.

BETH MOORE

If our charities do not at all pinch or hamper us, I should say they are too small. There ought to be things we should like to do and cannot do because our charitable expenditure excludes them.

C. S. LEWIS

Faithful servants never retire. You can retire from your career, but you will never retire from serving God.

RICK WARREN

REMEMBER THIS

A good steward knows that everything comes from God, and that God's blessings are inevitably bestowed upon those who are good stewards of the gifts He has entrusted to them.

GET PRACTICAL

Today, examine the quality of your stewardship. How are you managing the resources that God has entrusted to your care? And how are you managing your time?

A CONVERSATION STARTER

Talk to a friend about ways you can become a more effective steward of the resources God has entrusted to your care. And while you're at it, talk about the blessings that your family members will receive when they are faithful stewards of God's gifts.

NOTES TO YOURSELF ABOUT STEWARDSHIP AND SERVICE

Make a list of the things you need to do to become a more effective manager of the resources that the Creator has placed in your care. Jot down specific ways you and your family members can serve more and share more.

10

THE QUESTION

It's hard for me to forgive the people who have hurt me. And sometimes it's even hard to forgive close family members. What does the Bible say about that?

THE ANSWER

God's Word instructs you to forgive others, no exceptions. Forgiveness is its own reward and bitterness is its own punishment, so guard your words and your thoughts accordingly. And forgive everybody, starting with your family members, as quickly as you can.

There is always room for more loving forgiveness within our homes.

JAMES DOBSON

THE POWER OF FORGIVENESS

Judge not, and you shall not be judged.
Condemn not, and you shall not be condemned.
Forgive, and you will be forgiven.

LUKE 6:37 NKJV

Our families are precious gifts from our Father in heaven. If we are to be the righteous believers that God intends, we must care for our families, we must love our families, we must make time for our families, and, on occasion, we must forgive our families.

When we are injured by those we love, the pain we feel may be particularly intense. So, the sooner we can move beyond our feelings of disappointment and anger, the better. From a psychological perspective, the act of forgiving relieves you of some very heavy mental baggage: persistent feelings of hatred, anger, and regret. More importantly, the act of forgiveness brings with it a spiritual blessing, a knowledge that you have honored your heavenly Father by obeying His commandments. Simply put, forgiveness is a gift that you give yourself by giving it to someone else. When you make the choice to forgive, everybody wins, including you.

No family is perfect, and neither is yours. Despite the inevitable challenges, obligations, and hurt feelings of family life, your clan is God's blessing to you. So when it's time to forgive your loved ones, don't delay. That little band of men, women, kids, and babies is a priceless treasure on temporary loan from the Father above. Give thanks to the Giver for the gift of family . . . and act accordingly.

MORE FROM GOD'S WORD

Blessed are the merciful,
because they will be shown mercy.
MATTHEW 5:7 NIV

And whenever you stand praying,
if you have anything against anyone,
forgive him, so that your Father in heaven
may also forgive you your wrongdoing.
MARK 11:25 HCSB

And be kind to one another,
tenderhearted, forgiving one another,
just as God in Christ forgave you.
EPHESIANS 4:32 NKJV

Above all, love each other deeply,
because love covers a multitude of sins.
1 PETER 4:8 NIV

But I say to you, love your enemies
and pray for those who persecute you.
MATTHEW 5:44 NASB

MORE THOUGHTS ABOUT FORGIVENESS

The miraculous thing about being a family is that in the last analysis, we are each dependent on one another and God, woven together by mercy given and mercy received.

BARBARA JOHNSON

Forgiveness is the precondition of love.

CATHERINE MARSHALL

Forgiveness does not change the past, but it does enlarge the future.

DAVID JEREMIAH

In one bold stroke, forgiveness obliterates the past and permits us to enter the land of new beginnings.

BILLY GRAHAM

Forgiveness is an act of the will, and the will can function regardless of the temperature of the heart.

CORRIE TEN BOOM

REMEMBER THIS

God commands us to love all people, regardless of their personality styles. And the Lord makes no exceptions for family members. So don't be quick to judge your loved ones. Instead, be quick to forgive them. And remember that the Lord's instructions about forgiveness are commandments, not suggestions.

GET PRACTICAL

Whenever you speak, choose your words carefully. Harsh words are easy to speak and impossible to retrieve, so think before you speak.

A CONVERSATION STARTER

Talk to a friend about the rewards of forgiving and the costs of not forgiving.

NOTES TO YOURSELF ABOUT PEOPLE YOU NEED TO FORGIVE

Make a list of the people you still need to forgive. Then, ask God to cleanse your heart of bitterness, animosity, and regret. If you ask Him sincerely and often, He will respond.

11

THE QUESTION

Sometimes, it's hard to convince my loved ones
that worship is an important part
of family life. What does the Bible teach
us about the importance of worship?

THE ANSWER

Time and again the Bible teaches us
that it pays to praise the Lord. So the best way
for you and your family to worship God is to
worship Him sincerely and often. When you
genuinely strengthen your commitment to God,
you'll strengthen your family ties too.

Every Christian family ought to be, as it were,
a little church, consecrated to Christ, and wholly
influenced and governed by His rules.

JONATHAN EDWARDS

FAMILY WORSHIP

Worship the Lord with gladness. Come before him, singing with joy. Acknowledge that the Lord is God! He made us, and we are his. We are his people, the sheep of his pasture.

Psalm 100:2–3 NLT

All of mankind is engaged in worship of one kind or another. The question is not whether we worship, but what we worship. Some of us choose to worship God. The result is a plentiful harvest of joy, peace, and abundance. Others distance themselves from God by foolishly worshiping things of this earth such as fame, fortune, or personal gratification. To do so is a terrible mistake with eternal consequences.

Whenever we place our love for material possessions above our love for God—or when we yield to the countless temptations of this world—we find ourselves engaged in a struggle between good and evil, a clash between God and Satan. Our responses to these struggles have implications that echo throughout our families and throughout our communities.

How can we ensure that we cast our lot with God? We do so, in part, by the practice of regular, purposeful worship with our families. When we worship God faithfully and fervently, we are blessed. When we fail to worship God, for whatever reason, we forfeit the spiritual gifts that He intends for us.

We must worship our heavenly Father, not just with our words, but also with deeds. We must honor Him, praise Him, and obey Him. As we seek to find purpose and meaning for our lives, we must first seek His purpose and His will. For believers, God comes first. Always first.

MORE FROM GOD'S WORD

I was glad when they said unto me,
Let us go into the house of the Lord.

Psalm 122:1 KJV

For where two or three are gathered together
in My name, I am there among them.

Matthew 18:20 HCSB

God is spirit, and those who worship Him
must worship in spirit and truth.

John 4:24 HCSB

Happy are those who hear the joyful
call to worship, for they will walk in the light
of your presence, Lord.

Psalm 89:15 NLT

Remember the Sabbath day, to keep it holy.

Exodus 20:8 NKJV

MORE THOUGHTS ABOUT WORSHIP

Living life with a consistent spiritual walk deeply influences those we love most.

VONETTE BRIGHT

Worship is an inward reverence, the bowing down of the soul in the presence of God.

ELIZABETH GEORGE

Worship in the truest sense takes place only when our full attention is on God—His glory, majesty, love, and compassion.

BILLY GRAHAM

We must worship in truth. Worship is not just an emotional exercise but a response of the heart built on truth about God.

ERWIN LUTZER

Even the most routine part of your day can be a spiritual act of worship.

SARAH YOUNG

REMEMBER THIS

When you and your loved ones worship the Lord with praise on your lips and love in your heart, He will guide your steps and bless your family.

GET PRACTICAL

Worship reminds you of the awesome power of God. So worship Him daily, and allow Him to work through you every day of the week.

A CONVERSATION STARTER

Talk to a friend about the ways that God blesses you and your family when you worship Him sincerely and often.

NOTES TO YOURSELF ABOUT WORSHIP

Make a list of the things you like most about worship. Then, consider specific things you can do to enhance the worship experience for yourself and your family.

12
THE QUESTION

During tough times, I need courage,
and I know that my family members need it, too.
But sometimes courage is in short supply.
Where can we find it?

THE ANSWER

When tough times arrive (and they will), you and your family should turn your fears over to God. You should trust God to do His part, and then you should get busy doing your part to face—and resolve—your problems. In other words, you should work as if everything depended on you and pray as if everything depended on Him.

Adversity is not simply a tool. It is God's most effective tool for the advancement of our spiritual lives. The circumstances and events that we see as setbacks are oftentimes the very things that launch us into periods of intense spiritual growth. Once we begin to understand this, and accept it as a spiritual fact of life, adversity becomes easier to bear.

Charles Stanley

WHEN TIMES ARE TOUGH

God blesses those who patiently endure testing and temptation. Afterward they will receive the crown of life that God has promised to those who love him.

James 1:12 NLT

Tough times. Disappointments. Hardship. Pain. These experiences are the inevitable cost that each of us must pay for being human. When we're faced with these hardships, we may feel anxious or afraid. Thankfully, we must never encounter adversity alone. God is always with us.

When we are fearful, God stands ready and willing to protect us. Our responsibility, of course, is to ask Him for protection. When we call upon Him in prayer, He will answer—in His own time and in His own way.

If you find yourself enduring difficult circumstances, remember that God remains in His heaven. If you become discouraged with the direction of your day or your life, turn your thoughts and prayers to Him. He is a God of possibility, not negativity. He will guide you and your family through your difficulties and beyond them. And then, with a renewed spirit of optimism and hope, you can thank the Giver for gifts that are simply too numerous to count.

God's love for you never changes, and neither does His support. From the cradle to the grave, He has promised to give you the strength to meet the challenges of life. He has promised to guide you and protect you if you let Him. But He also expects you to do your part. Today provides yet another opportunity to partake in the strength that only God can provide. You do so by attuning your heart to Him through prayer, obedience, and trust. Life can be challenging, but fear not. Whatever your challenge, God can give you the strength to face it and overcome it. Let Him.

MORE FROM GOD'S WORD

We are hard-pressed on every side, yet not crushed; we are perplexed, but not in despair.

2 Corinthians 4:8 NKJV

The Lord is my shepherd; I shall not want.

Psalm 23:1 KJV

He heals the brokenhearted
and binds up their wounds.

Psalm 147:3 HCSB

I called to the Lord in my distress;
I called to my God. From His temple
He heard my voice.

2 Samuel 22:7 HCSB

The Lord is my rock, my fortress, and my deliverer,
my God, my mountain where I seek refuge.
My shield, the horn of my salvation,
my stronghold, my refuge, and my Savior.

2 Samuel 22:2–3 HCSB

MORE THOUGHTS ABOUT TOUGH TIMES

No faith is so precious as that which triumphs over adversity.

C. H. Spurgeon

The sermon of your life in tough times ministers to people more powerfully than the most eloquent speaker.

Bill Bright

The great thing with unhappy times is to take them bit by bit, hour by hour, like an illness. It is seldom the present, the exact present, that is unbearable.

C. S. Lewis

God is in control. He may not take away trials or make detours for us, but He strengthens us through them.

Billy Graham

Often the trials we mourn are really gateways into the good things we long for.

Hannah Whitall Smith

REMEMBER THIS

When we experiencer the inevitable disappointments and hardships of life, we do so with the ultimate armor—God's promises. When we ask for His guidance, He leads us along the right path—His path.

GET PRACTICAL

If your life has been turned upside down, you may find yourself searching for something new: a different direction, a new purpose, or a fresh start. As you make your plans, be sure to consult God. He never leaves you. Your task is to pray, to listen, and to follow His lead.

A CONVERSATION STARTER

Talk to a friend about ways that tough times help you grow spiritually and emotionally.

NOTES TO YOURSELF ABOUT OVERCOMING TOUGH TIMES

Write down your ideas about the best ways to muster the courage and faithfulness you'll need whenever you encounter tough times.

13

THE QUESTION

Sometimes, it's easy for me to become angry. What does the Bible say about anger?

THE ANSWER

We are warned time and again that anger is only one letter away from danger. So the next time you're tempted to lose your cool or say something you'll probably regret, walk away before you get carried away.

Never underestimate anger's destructive power.

BILLY GRAHAM

BEYOND ANGER

Do not let the sun go down on your anger, and do not give the devil an opportunity.

EPHESIANS 4:26–27 NASB

Angry outbursts or pent-up resentments can be harmful, hurtful, and dangerous to your family's spiritual health. Whenever your thoughts are hijacked by angry emotions, you forfeit the peace and perspective that might otherwise be yours. And to make matters worse, angry thoughts can cause you and your family members to behave in irrational, self-destructive ways.

1 Peter 5:8–9 warns "Stay alert! Watch out for your great enemy, the devil. He prowls around like a roaring lion, looking for someone to devour. Stand firm against him, and be strong in your faith." (NLT). And of this you can be sure: Your adversary will use an unforgiving heart, and the inevitable anger that dwells within it, to sabotage your life, your faith, and your family. To be safe, you must cleanse your heart, and you must forgive everybody as soon as possible, if not sooner. In other words, you must say yes to God, yes to mercy, yes to love, and no to anger.

MORE FROM GOD'S WORD

A hot-tempered man stirs up conflict,
but a man slow to anger calms strife.

Proverbs 15:18 HCSB

Everyone must be quick to hear, slow to speak,
and slow to anger, for man's anger does not
accomplish God's righteousness.

James 1:19-20 HCSB

He who is slow to wrath has great understanding,
but he who is impulsive exalts folly.

Proverbs 14:29 NKJV

But now you must also put away all the following:
anger, wrath, malice, slander,
and filthy language from your mouth.

Colossians 3:8 HCSB

But I tell you that anyone who is angry
with his brother or sister will be subject to judgment.

Matthew 5:22 NIV

MORE THOUGHTS ABOUT ANGER

Calm and peaceful, the home should be the one place where people are certain they will be welcomed, received, protected, and loved.

Ed Young

We must meet our disappointments, our malicious enemies, our provoking friends, our trials of every sort, with an attitude of surrender and trust. We must rise above them in Christ so they lose their power to harm us.

Hannah Whitall Smith

Anger is the noise of the soul; the unseen irritant of the heart; the relentless invader of silence.

Max Lucado

Anger and bitterness—whatever the cause—only end up hurting us. Turn that anger over to Christ.

Billy Graham

When you strike out in anger, you may miss the other person, but you will always hit yourself.

Jim Gallery

REMEMBER THIS

Emotions are highly contagious and angry encounters almost never have happy endings. So, if someone is ranting, raving, or worse, you have the right to leave the scene of the argument.

GET PRACTICAL

When you're beginning to feel angry, slow yourself down, take a deep breath, and walk away from the scene of the argument. It's better to walk away—and keep walking—than it is to speak angry words that you'll soon regret.

A CONVERSATION STARTER

Talk to a friend about productive ways to deal with—and productive ways to express—angry feelings and pent-up emotions.

NOTES TO YOURSELF ABOUT ANGER

Write down your thoughts about the inevitable problems that result from anger that's either expressed in inappropriate ways or held inside.

14

THE QUESTION

Sometimes, when times are hard and the headlines are disheartening, it's hard for me and my loved ones to be optimistic. What does the Bible say about optimism and hope?

THE ANSWER

God's Word promises that if you've given your heart to Jesus, your eternal future is secure. So even when times are tough, you and your loved ones can be joyful, hopeful, and optimistic. God created you in His own image, and He wants you to experience joy, contentment, peace, and abundance. But, He will not force you to experience these things; you must claim them for yourself. If you want to defeat your anxieties and fears, you'll need the right kind of attitude—the positive kind.

Gratitude unlocks the fullness of life. It turns what we have into enough, and more. It turns denial into acceptance, chaos to order, confusion to clarity. It can turn a meal into a feast, a house into a home, a stranger into a friend. Gratitude makes sense of our past, brings peace for today, and creates a vision for tomorrow.

Melody Beattie

THE POWER OF OPTIMISM

Let us hold on to the confession of our hope without wavering, for He who promised is faithful.

HEBREWS 10:23 HCSB

Of course you've heard the saying, "Life is what you make it." And although that statement may seem very trite, it's also very true. You can choose a life filled to the brim with frustration and fear, or you can choose a life of abundance and peace. That choice is up to you—and only you—and it depends, to a surprising extent, upon your attitude.

What's your attitude today? And what's the prevailing attitude of the people who live under your roof? Are you fearful, angry, bored, or worried? Are you pessimistic, perplexed, pained, and perturbed? If so, God wants to have a little talk with you.

God created you (and yours) in His own image, and He wants you (and yours) to experience joy, contentment, peace, and abundance. But, God will not force you to experience these things; you must claim them for yourselves.

God has given you and your family members free will, including the ability to influence the direction and the tone of your thoughts. And here's how God wants you to direct those thoughts:

Finally brothers, whatever is true, whatever is honorable, whatever is just, whatever is pure, whatever is lovely, whatever is commendable—if there is any moral excellence and if there is any praise—dwell on these things" (Philippians 4:8 HCSB).

The quality of your attitude will help determine the quality of your life, so you must guard your thoughts accordingly. If you and your loved ones decide to approach life with a healthy mixture of realism and optimism, you'll be rewarded. And when is the best time to start reaping the rewards of positive thinking? Right now, of course, if not sooner.

MORE FROM GOD'S WORD

The LORD is my light and my salvation—
whom should I fear? The LORD is the stronghold
of my life—of whom should I be afraid?

PSALM 27:1 HCSB

This hope we have as an anchor of the soul,
a hope both sure and steadfast.

HEBREWS 6:19 NASB

"I say this because I know what I am planning
for you," says the LORD. "I have good
plans for you, not plans to hurt you.
I will give you hope and a good future."

JEREMIAH 29:11 NCV

Make me to hear joy and gladness.

PSALM 51:8 KJV

Focus on this one thing: Forgetting the past
and looking forward to what lies ahead.

PHILIPPIANS 3:13 NLT NLT

MORE THOUGHTS ABOUT OPTIMISM

Positive thinking will let you do everything better than negative thinking will.

ZIG ZIGLAR

Never yield to gloomy anticipation. Place your hope and confidence in God. He has no record of failure.

LETTIE COWMAN

Developing a positive attitude means working continually to find what is uplifting and encouraging.

BARBARA JOHNSON

All things work together for good. Fret not, nor fear!

LETTIE COWMAN

Live in the present and make the most of your opportunities to enjoy your family and friends.

BARBARA JOHNSON

REMEMBER THIS

As a Christian, you have every reason to be optimistic. So, don't give up on God. And remember: He will never give up on you or your family.

GET PRACTICAL

It pays to be optimistic, and it pays to celebrate. So today and every day, remember to celebrate God's gifts, starting with your family. Learn to think realistically about yourself, your family, and your situation while making a conscious effort to focus on your hopes, not your fears.

A CONVERSATION STARTER

Talk to a friend about the potential rewards of optimism and the potential dangers of pessimism.

NOTES TO YOURSELF ABOUT THE REWARDS OF OPTIMISM

Write down why you think it's important (and helpful) to be optimistic about your faith, your family, and your life.

15

THE QUESTION

The world is filled with distractions and temptations that are a constant threat to my family. What should I do?

THE ANSWER

Of course there is darkness in this world, and temptations galore. But God's light can overpower any darkness. So make sure that your family's life—and faith—is built on the firm foundation of God's Word. Make sure that your children have plenty of advance warning (from you) about the dangers they will encounter. And keep praying that everyone in your clan will have the wisdom and the strength to avoid the darkness.

Our Creator, who divided the year into seasons and the days into mornings and nights, also divided people into families. He created this gift of a structure to offer stability and loving security in the midst of an unstable and insecure world.

Carol Kuykendall

RESISTING THE WORLD'S PRIORITIES

And do not be conformed to this world,
but be transformed by the renewing of your mind,
that you may prove what is that good
and acceptable and perfect will of God.

Romans 12:2 NKJV

We live in the world, but we should not worship it. Our duty is to place God first and everything else second. But because we are fallible beings with imperfect faith, placing God in His rightful place is often difficult. In fact, at every turn, or so it seems, we are tempted to do otherwise. If you wish to possess a comfortable conscience and a peaceful soul, you must distance yourself, at least in part, from the temptations and distractions of modern-day society. But distancing yourself isn't easy, especially when so many societal forces are struggling to capture your attention, your participation, and your money.

The twenty-first-century world is a noisy, distracting place filled with countless opportunities to stray from God's will. The world seems to cry out to you and your family, "Worship me with your time, your money, your energy, and your thoughts!" But God commands otherwise. He instructs you to worship Him and to love your neighbors; everything else must be secondary.

The world's treasures are difficult to find and difficult to keep; God's treasures are ever-present and everlasting. Which treasures, then, will you claim as your own?

MORE FROM GOD'S WORD

Pure and undefiled religion before our God and Father is this: to look after orphans and widows in their distress and to keep oneself unstained by the world.

James 1:27 HCSB

Set your mind on the things above, not on the things that are on earth.

Colossians 3:2 NASB

Do you not know that friendship with the world is hostility toward God? So whoever wants to be the world's friend becomes God's enemy.

James 4:4 HCSB

For our citizenship is in heaven, from which also we eagerly wait for a Savior, the Lord Jesus Christ.

Philippians 3:20 NASB

No one can serve two masters.
For you will hate one and love the other;
you will be devoted to one and despise the other.
You cannot serve God and be enslaved to money.

Luke 16:13 NLT

MORE THOUGHTS ABOUT RESISTING WORLDLINESS

We need more love for the word and less love for the world.

R. G. Lee

We live in a hostile world that constantly seeks to pull us away from God.

Billy Graham

If you are a Christian, you are not a citizen of this world trying to get to heaven; you are a citizen of heaven making your way through this world.

Vance Havner

We must strengthen our commitment to model strong families ourselves, to live by godly priorities in a culture where self so often supersedes commitment to others. And, as we not only model but assertively reach out to help others, we must realize that even huge societal problems are solved one person at a time.

Chuck Colson

No other structure can replace the family. Without it, our children have no moral foundation. Without it, they become moral illiterates whose only law is self.

Chuck Colson

REMEMBER THIS

The world is designed to distract you from the plan God has for you and your loved ones. Satan wants to distance you from your faith. So you must guard yourself against the temptations and distractions that the world has to offer. When you do, you'll be blessed.

GET PRACTICAL

The world wants to monopolize your time and rearrange your priorities. But God wants you to invest ample time caring for your family. Sometimes you must say yes to your family's priorities even if it means saying no to the world's priorities.

A CONVERSATION STARTER

Talk to a friend about some of the ways that the world invades your lives, disrupts your families, and attacks your faith.

NOTES TO YOURSELF ABOUT RESISTING WORLDLINESS

Write down specific dangers of worldliness and specific things you can do to protect yourself and your family.

16

THE QUESTION

When I worry about my family—
or about anything else, for that matter—
what should I do? And where should I turn?

THE ANSWER

First, remember that God is in control and that He loves you. Then, carefully divide your areas of concern into two categories: those things you can control and those you cannot control. Once you've done so, spend your time working to resolve the things you can control, and entrust everything else to the Lord.

Do not worry about tomorrow.
This is not a suggestion, but a command.

Sarah Young

ABOVE AND BEYOND WORRY

Therefore do not worry about tomorrow,
for tomorrow will worry about its own things.
Sufficient for the day is its own trouble.

MATTHEW 6:34 NKJV

Because you and your family members have the ability to think, you also have the ability to worry. Even if you're a very faithful Christians, you may be plagued by occasional periods of discouragement and doubt. Even though you trust God's promise of salvation—even though you sincerely believe in God's love and protection—you may find yourself upset by the countless details of everyday life.

Where is the best place to take your worries? Take them to God. Take your troubles to Him; take your fears to Him; take your doubts to Him; take your weaknesses to Him; take your sorrows to Him . . . and leave them all there. Seek protection from the One who offers you eternal salvation—build your spiritual house upon the Rock that cannot be moved.

Perhaps you or your loved ones are concerned about the future, or about your relationships, or about your finances. Or perhaps you are simply "worriers" by nature. If so, remember that God still sits in His heaven and that you are His beloved children. Then, perhaps, you will worry a little less and trust God a little more, and that's as it should be because God is trustworthy, and you are protected.

MORE FROM GOD'S WORD

Cast your burden on the Lord,
And He shall sustain you; He shall never permit the righteous to be moved.

Psalm 55:22 NKJV

Do not be anxious about anything, but in every situation, by prayer and petition, with thanksgiving, present your requests to God.

Philippians 4:6 NIV

Peace I leave with you;
My peace I give to you;
not as the world gives do I give to you.
Do not let your heart be troubled,
nor let it be fearful.

John 14:27 NASB

Let not your heart be troubled;
you believe in God, believe also in Me.

John 14:1 NKJV

Cast all your anxiety on him
because he cares for you.

1 Peter 5:7 NIV

MORE THOUGHTS ABOUT LIVING ABOVE ANXIETY AND WORRY

Worry and anxiety are sand in
the machinery of life; faith is the oil.

E. Stanley Jones

Do not hide from your fear or pretend that it isn't
there. Anxiety that you hide in the recesses
of your heart will give birth to fear of fear.

Sarah Young

Look around you and you'll be distressed;
look within yourself and you'll be depressed;
look at Jesus, and you'll be at rest!

Corrie ten Boom

Knowing that God is faithful, it really
helps me to not be captivated by worry.

Josh McDowell

Today is the tomorrow you
worried about yesterday.

Billy Graham

REMEMBER THIS

You have worries, but God has solutions. Your challenge is to trust Him to solve the problems that are simply too big for you to resolve on your own.

GET PRACTICAL

Divide your areas of concern into two categories: those you can control and those you can't. Focus on the former and refuse to waste time or energy worrying about the latter.

A CONVERSATION STARTER

Talk to a friend about ways to trust God more and worry less.

NOTES TO YOURSELF ABOUT LIVING ABOVE ANXIETY AND WORRY

Write down a few practical things you can do to overcome anxiety and worry. And while you're at it, don't forget that spending time with God every day can help you worry less and trust Him more.

17

THE QUESTION

What does the Bible say about God's love? And what should His love mean to me and my family?

THE ANSWER

Of course we mortals can never begin to understand or comprehend the Creator. But the Bible teaches us this much: God is love. And we should find comfort in that fact. When all else fails, God's love does not. You and your loved ones can always depend upon God's love; He is your ultimate protection.

God expresses His love by putting us in a family.

CHARLES STANLEY

GOD LOVES YOUR FAMILY

And we have known and believed the love that God has for us. God is love, and he who abides in love abides in God, and God in him.

1 John 4:16 NKJV

God loves you and your family. He loves you more than you can imagine; His affection is deeper than you can fathom. God made you in His own image and gave you salvation through the person of His Son Jesus Christ. And as a result, you and your loved ones have an important decision to make. You must decide what to do about God's love: you can return it . . . or not.

When you accept the love that flows from the heart of God, you are transformed. When you embrace God's love, you feel differently about yourself, your family, your neighbors, your community, your church, and your world. When you open your heart to God's love, you will feel compelled to share God's message—and His compassion—with others.

God's heart is overflowing with love for you and yours. Accept that love. Return that love. And share that love. Today.

MORE FROM GOD'S WORD

The Lord's lovingkindnesses indeed never cease, for His compassions never fail. They are new every morning. Great is Your faithfulness.

Lamentations 3:22–23 NASB

Give thanks to Him and praise His name.
For Yahweh is good, and His love is eternal;
His faithfulness endures through all generations.

Psalm 100:4–5 HCSB

For God so loved the world, that he gave his only begotten Son, that whosoever believeth in him should not perish, but have everlasting life.

John 3:16 KJV

We love him, because he first loved us.

1 John 4:19 KJV

For He is gracious and compassionate, slow to anger, rich in faithful love.

Joel 2:13 HCSB

MORE THOUGHTS ABOUT GOD'S LOVE

There is no limit to God. There is no limit to His power. There is no limit to His love. There is no limit to His mercy.

Billy Graham

The greatest sense of love, which is available for us at all times, is God's love.

Stormie Omartian

God is the giver, and we are the receivers. And His richest gifts are bestowed not upon those who do the greatest things, but upon those who accept His abundance and His grace.

Hannah Whitall Smith

God loves you and wants you to experience peace and life—abundant and eternal.

Billy Graham

Jesus: the proof of God's love.

Phillip Yancey

REMEMBER THIS

When all else fails, God's love does not. You can always depend upon God's love, and He is always your ultimate protection. Your assignment is to return His love and share it with your family and with the world.

GET PRACTICAL

Building a meaningful relationship with God takes time. So it's important to spend time with Him every day, not just on Sundays. That's why you need a regularly scheduled meeting with him every morning.

—∞—

A CONVERSATION STARTER

Talk to a friend about the blessings that are yours whenever you open your heart to God. And while you're at it, discuss ways that God's love for you can have a meaningful impact on your family.

NOTES TO YOURSELF ABOUT GOD'S LOVE FOR YOUR FAMILY

Write down specific ways that God has blessed you and your family.

18

THE QUESTION

Sometimes I feel stuck, and sometimes,
I feel confused. How can I discover
God's purpose for my life?

THE ANSWER

God's plans for you are unfolding day by day.
If you keep your eyes and your heart open,
He'll reveal those plans. God has big things
in store for you, but He may have quite a few
lessons to teach you before you are fully
prepared to do His will and fulfill His purposes.

The only true source of meaning in life is found
in love for God and his son Jesus Christ, and love
for mankind, beginning with our own families.

James Dobson

FINDING PURPOSE THROUGH FAMILY

And whatever you do, do it heartily, as to the Lord and not to men.

COLOSSIANS 3:23 NKJV

As you consider God's purpose for your life, you must also consider how your plans will affect the most important people that God has entrusted to your care: your loved ones. God intends that we honor Him by honoring our families. We honor our families by giving them our love, our support, our advice, our cooperation, and, when needed, our discipline. And there's no getting around it: these matters require significant investments of time.

Life is best lived on purpose. And purpose, like everything else in the universe, begins with God. Whether you realize it or not, God has a plan for your life, a divine calling, a direction in which He is leading you. When you welcome the Lord into your heart and establish a genuine relationship with Him, He will begin, in time, to make His purposes known. Sometimes, the Lord's intentions will be clear to you; other times, His plan will seem uncertain at best. But even on those difficult days when you are unsure which way to turn, you must never lose sight of these overriding facts: God created you for a reason; He has important work for you to do; and He's waiting patiently for you to do it.

God has a plan for your life and a purpose that only you can fulfill. An important part of that plan—in truth a crucial part of the plan—is the comfort, support, and love you give to you family. Your family needs you, and you need them. And the next move is yours.

MORE FROM GOD'S WORD

We have also received an inheritance in Him,
predestined according to the purpose
of the One who works out everything
in agreement with the decision of His will.

Ephesians 1:11 HCSB

We must do the works of Him who sent Me while
it is day. Night is coming when no one can work.

John 9:4 HCSB

For we are His creation, created in Christ Jesus
for good works, which God prepared ahead
of time so that we should walk in them.

Ephesians 2:10 HCSB

Whether you eat or drink,
or whatever you do,
do it all for the glory of God

1 Corinthians 10:31 NLT

For we are God's coworkers.
You are God's field, God's building.

1 Corinthians 3:9 HCSB

MORE THOUGHTS ABOUT PURPOSE

As the first community to which a person is attached and the first authority under which a person learns to live, the family establishes society's most basic values.

Charles Colson

I cannot overemphasize the importance of parental support and love during the formative years of life. A child's sense of security and well-being is primarily rooted in the stability of his home and family.

James Dobson

The family circle is the supreme conductor of Christianity.

Henry Drummond

More than any other single factor in a person's formative years, family life forges character.

John Maxwell

The mind of Christ is to be learned in the family. Strength of character may be acquired at work, but beauty of character is learned at home.

Henry Drummond

REMEMBER THIS

God has big things in store for you, but He may have quite a few lessons to teach you before you are fully prepared to fulfill His purposes. So be patient, be watchful, keep working, and keep praying. Divine help is on the way.

GET PRACTICAL

Grab a sheet of paper and jot down a brief, personal, mission statement. But don't stop there. Keep refining your mission statement until you're confident that it reflects your talents, your opportunities, your passion, and your obligations to your family.

A CONVERSATION STARTER

Talk to a friend about specific ways you can learn God's purpose for you and follow His path.

NOTES TO YOURSELF ABOUT GOD'S PURPOSE

Write down a few things you feel God may be calling you to do during the next 12 months. Are you preparing yourself to answer His call? If so, congratulations. If not, jot down specific things you can do to fulfill God's purpose for you and your family.

19

THE QUESTION

Sometimes it seems like the media is attacking my family. What should I do?

THE ANSWER

The modern media is sending out messages that are dangerous to your family's physical, emotional, and spiritual health. You, as a responsible parent, must decide which messages and which images are appropriate for your family. The responsibility is yours and yours alone, not that of television executives or web-page designers.

The media relentlessly proclaim bad news: for breakfast, lunch, and dinner. A steady diet of their fare will sicken you. Instead of focusing on fickle, ever-changing news broadcasts, tune in to the living Word.

Sarah Young

BEWARE OF THE MEDIA

Stay alert! Watch out for your great enemy, the devil. He prowls around like a roaring lion, looking for someone to devour. Stand firm against him, and be strong in your faith.

1 Peter 5:8–9 NLT

If you and your loved ones have acquired the bad habit of watching whatever happens to pop up on you family's TV screen, it's time to rethink the way you control your clicker. Most television networks (as well as the other forms of popular media) can be dangerous to your emotional and spiritual health.

The media is working around the clock in an attempt to rearrange your family's priorities in ways that are definitely not in your best interests. The media is trying to teach your family that physical appearance is all-important, that material possessions should be acquired at any cost, and that the world operates independently of God's laws. But guess what? Those messages are lies.

In the pursuit of profits, the media glamorizes violence, exploits suffering, and sensationalizes sex, all in the name of ratings (translated: money).

So here's a question for you and your family: will you control what appears on your TV screen, or will you be controlled by it? If you're willing to take complete control over the images that appear inside the four walls of your home, you'll be doing yourselves a king-sized favor. So forget the media hype, and pay attention to God. Stand up for Him and be counted, not just in church where it's relatively easy to be a Christian, but also when you're deciding what to watch. You owe it to your Creator, and you owe it to yourselves.

MORE FROM GOD'S WORD

Do not be mismatched with unbelievers. For what partnership is there between righteousness and lawlessness? Or what fellowship does light have with darkness?

2 Corinthians 6:14 HCSB

Dear friend, do not imitate what is evil, but what is good. The one who does good is of God; the one who does evil has not seen God.

3 John 1:11 HCSB

Set your mind on the things above, not on the things that are on earth.

Colossians 3:2 NASB

Let no one deceive himself. If anyone among you seems to be wise in this age, let him become a fool that he may become wise. For the wisdom of this world is foolishness with God. For it is written, "He catches the wise in their own craftiness."

1 Corinthians 3:18–19 NKJV

MORE THOUGHTS ABOUT POPULAR MEDIA

Our fight is not against any physical enemy; it is against organizations and powers that are spiritual. We must struggle against sin all our lives, but we are assured we will win.

CORRIE TEN BOOM

Reading news without reading the Bible will inevitably lead to an unbalanced life, an anxious spirit, a worried and depressed soul.

BILL BRIGHT

Television is like a thief. It steals time; it kills initiative; it destroys relationships.

EDWIN LOUIS COLE

There are two great forces at work in the world today: the unlimited power of God and the limited power of Satan.

CORRIE TEN BOOM

The Christian life isn't a playground but a battlefield.

BILLY GRAHAM

REMEMBER THIS

If you're serious about making God the cornerstone of your home, you must make the effort to watch and listen to programming that reinforces the principles set forth in God's Word. And while you're at it, you must be distrustful of media messages that are harmful to your family's spiritual or emotional health.

GET PRACTICAL

Pay careful attention to the media images that are viewed in your home. And be sure to reject those images that are inappropriate for your family.

A CONVERSATION STARTER

Talk to a friend about the dangers, temptations, and distractions of modern media.

NOTES TO YOURSELF ABOUT YOUR RELATIONSHIP WITH THE MEDIA

Write down an estimate of the amount of time you spend each day consuming media content. Then, evaluate the quality of the media you consume and the things you could do if you spent less time peering into all those screens.

20

THE QUESTION

What does the Bible say about putting God first in my own life? And how can I influence family members to put the Lord first in their own lives?

THE ANSWER

God's Word is clear: if you put Him first in every aspect of your life, you'll be blessed. But if you relegate God to a position of lesser importance, you'll distance yourself from His blessings. And as you attempt to influence your family, remember that the words you speak may have some impact on others, but not nearly as much impact as the life you choose to live.

Jesus Christ is the first and last, author and finisher, beginning and end, alpha and omega, and by Him all other things hold together. He must be first or nothing. God never comes next!

VANCE HAVNER

PUTTING GOD FIRST IN THE LIFE OF YOUR FAMILY

You shall have no other gods before Me.

Exodus 20:3 NKJV

As you fulfill the responsibilities of caring for your family, what is your top priority? Do you and your loved ones strive to place God first in every aspect of your lives, or do you usually focus on other priorities? The answer to this simple question will determine the quality and the direction of your own life and the lives of your family members.

As you contemplate your family's relationship with God, remember this: all of mankind is engaged in the practice of worship. Some families choose to worship God and, as a result, they reap the joy that He intends for His children. Other families distance themselves from God by worshiping such things as earthly possessions or personal gratification, and when they do so, they suffer.

In the book of Exodus, God warns that we should place no gods before Him. Yet all too often, we place our Lord in second, third, or fourth place as we worship the gods of pride, possessions, prestige, or power.

When we place our desires for material possessions above our love for the Father—or when we yield to the inevitable temptations and complications of everyday life—we find ourselves engaged in a struggle that is similar to the one Jesus faced when He was tempted by Satan. In the wilderness, Satan offered Jesus earthly power and unimaginable riches, but Jesus turned Satan away and chose instead to worship God. We must do likewise by putting God first and by worshiping only Him.

Does God rule over your heart and your home? Make certain that the honest answer to this question is a resounding yes. In the collective life of every Christian family, God should come first—and it's up to you to make certain that He comes first at your house.

MORE FROM GOD'S WORD

With my whole heart I have sought You;
Oh, let me not wander from Your commandments!

PSALM 119:10 NKJV

Do not love the world or the things that belong
to the world. If anyone loves the world,
love for the Father is not in him.

1 JOHN 2:15 HCSB

No one can serve two masters.
For you will hate one and love the other;
you will be devoted to one and despise the other.
You cannot serve God and be enslaved to money.

LUKE 16:13 NLT

Jesus said to him, "'You shall love the LORD
your God with all your heart, with all your soul,
and with all your mind.' This is the first
and great commandment.

MATTHEW 22:37–38 NKJV

Be careful not to forget the LORD.

DEUTERONOMY 6:12 HCSB

MORE THOUGHTS ABOUT PUTTING GOD FIRST

Make God's will the focus of your life day by day. If you seek to please Him and Him alone, you'll find yourself satisfied with life.

Kay Arthur

A man's spiritual health is exactly proportional to his love for God.

C. S. Lewis

You must never sacrifice your relationship with God for the sake of a relationship with another person.

Charles Stanley

Fill up the spare moments of your life with praise and thanksgiving.

Sarah Young

Preoccupy my thoughts with your praise beginning today.

Joni Eareckson Tada

REMEMBER THIS

Put God first in every aspect of your life. And while you're at it, put Him first in every aspect of your family's life too.

GET PRACTICAL

Be expressive. Make certain that your own faith in God is expressed and demonstrated many times each day. Frequent expressions of worship and praise will make a big difference in the life of your child.

A CONVERSATION STARTER

Talk to a friend about the rewards of putting God first and the dangers of ignoring Him.

NOTES TO YOURSELF ABOUT PUTTING GOD FIRST IN YOUR FAMILY

Write down some specific ways you can put God first in your family.